D1111931

The
Entrepreneurial
Vocation

The Entrepreneurial Vocation

Robert A. Sirico

Introduction by William E. LaMothe

ACTONINSTITUTE

The Entrepreneurial Vocation

© 2001 by Acton Institute

Scripture quotations marked (NRSV) are taken from the New Revised Standard Version Bible, copyright © 1989 the Division of Christian Education of the National Council of the Churches of Christ in the United States of America. Used by permission. All rights reserved.

Scripture quotations marked (KJV) are taken from the King James Version.

ISBN 978-1-880595-20-6
CIP data is on file at the Library of Congress

ACTONINSTITUTE

98 E. Fulton
Grand Rapids, Michigan 49503
616.454.3080
www.acton.org

Printed in the United States of America

Contents

Introduction

To those of us who have spent most of our years in the business world, the title of this essay by Rev. Robert Sirico may sound a bit strange. In my own experience, the very word *vocation* generally meant a calling, which, in turn, usually implied a calling to life as a priest or nun, or as a clergyman or missionary. The question the title raises, then, is this: How do the concepts of entrepreneur and vocation come together and make sense?

In this essay, Father Sirico answers that question. The case can certainly be made that all entrepreneurs believe strongly enough in their ideas to accept the fact that those ideas convey a calling—a calling that spurs them on, often to risk everything to make it happen. If a product or service is successful, it fills a need for those buying it, and the entrepreneur may then go on to fame and riches. Even if a given product is unsuccessful, the entrepreneur can maintain confidence if he is convinced that God has chosen him to take on this kind of task as his life's work.

Father Sirico points out the need for entrepreneurs to have the moral framework within which to understand their efforts. This understanding helps the businessman to affirm the dignity of the enterprise that he has undertaken. It also imparts certain responsibilities to him; he cannot think of his business efforts without reference to the dictates of his conscience and the religious principles to which he adheres.

The essay also highlights the need for others, especially religious leaders, to recognize and appreciate the moral character of the entrepreneur's efforts. Many religious leaders are suspicious of the free enterprise system and of the entrepreneur. Father Sirico not only attempts to clarify the division between businessmen and clergy but also offers a way to bridge that gap. He does this by elucidating the Christian principles that are inherent to the entrepreneurial spirit.

Father Sirico is uniquely positioned to analyze the spheres of religion and business. As a member of the clergy, he has undergone the seminary experience and theological education and has worked as a paastor. He understands the requirements of social justice and exhibits a deep concern for those who have not been able to share in the wealth created by the market economy.

At the same time, he has been a student of the free enterprise system. He has written and spoken extensively on the excellence of a society that is both free and virtuous. He has also interacted with and guided business leaders. Father Sirico not only calls for the clergy to engage businessmen and vice versa—he initiates that encounter. I can testify on the basis of firsthand experience that his seminars for business executives are events that put into practice the principles outlined in this essay. I have greatly benefited from Father Sirico's reflections, which have led me to a better understanding of my role as a businessman and of the moral responsibilities that come with that calling.

It is my sincere hope that all entrepreneurs and business leaders (as well as others) will, through this essay, come to a better understanding of the role of entrepreneurship and its sublime dimension as a calling from God.

> William E. LaMothe
> Chairman Emeritus
> Kellogg Corporation

The Entrepreneurial Vocation

There was a time, in the not-too-distant past, when prejudice was an acceptable social posture. However, stereotypes, which typically function as shortcuts to knowledge, are today considered offensive. This is so, regardless of whether or not they elucidate a group characteristic. People ought not be judged merely by the associations they keep, without regard for their person or individual qualities. Such a tendency is objectionable to anyone with moral sensibilities.

Despite the laudable attitude of popular culture against prejudice of any form, there remains one group upon which an unofficial open season has been declared: entrepreneurs. One sees vivid evidence of this prejudice at nearly every turn, particularly in terms of popular forms of communication. Consider, for example, classic literary works (say, of Charles Dickens[1] or Sinclair Lewis[2]), television programs (such as *Dallas* or *Dynasty*), films (*The China Syndrome*, *Wall Street*, and some versions of *A Christmas Carol*), cartoon strips (such as *Doonesbury* and *Dilbert*), and even sermons in which entre-preneurs are depicted as greedy, immoral, and cutthroat.[3]

On the rare occasion when opinion makers, especially moral leaders, refrain from denouncing the "rapacious appetite" and the "obscene and conspicuous consumption" of these capitalists, about the best that one can expect is that business people be tolerated as a necessary evil. Most news editors, novelists, film producers, and clergy assume that commerce requires a broad and complicated network of controls to serve genuine human needs. Even friends of capitalism frequently display the same attitude. Religious leaders and critics of the market often suffer from confusion in their economic and moral thinking. This can be seen, for example, in their refusal to grant any moral sanction to the entrepreneur. Thus, instead of praising the entrepreneur as a person of ideas, an economic innovator, or a provider of capital, the average priest or minister thinks of people in business as carrying extra guilt. Why? For owning, controlling, or manipulating a disproportionate percentage of "society's" wealth.

While entrepreneurs should not be unfairly criticized for making money, they also must not be treated as victims of unjust discrimination who deserve a special blessing. How-ever, it is also true that their chosen profession deserves to be legitimized by their faith. The public must begin to acknowledge the value of the entrepreneurial vocation, the wise stewardship of talents, and the tangible contributions of entrepreneurs to society.

The consequences of a divorce between the world of business and the world of faith would be disastrous in both arenas. For the world of business, it would mean not acknowledging any values higher than expediency, profit, and utility, which would result in what has been described as bloody or savage capital-ism.[4] It would lead to a truncated view of consumers as well as of producers, whose sole value would be measured by utility. It does not require much imagination to gauge the effect such attitudes would exert on a wide range of social and civic norms.

Similarly, the preconceived notions of religious leaders must be challenged to avoid the charge of "being so heavenly minded they are no earthly good." For-getting that enterprise requires insight or intuition, and not merely a transcendent reference point directing it to the overall good of society, religious critics disregard the implicit spiritual dimension of enterprise.

Some moralists[5] seem to view business ethics as either an oxymoron or as an effort to subordinate what is intrinsically an ethically compromised mechanism to moral norms. To this way of thinking, ethics and business stand in fundamental tension with one another. However, I see matters differently. My work with an array of successful business leaders, extensive reading in the fields of economics and business ethics, and a fair amount of meditation and prayer on these matters have led me to the conclusion that *searching for excellence is the beginning of a search for God*. Put succinctly, the human thirst for the transcendent is what drives people to seek excellence, whether they acknowledge it or not. Nonetheless, this does not preclude our initial impulse and intuition from being a (divine) tug in the right direction. This is also the case with the human capacity for knowledge. Various philosophers and theologians contend that the human quest for knowledge reveals that human beings are ontologically oriented toward the truth. The human mind was originally designed to have an immediate awareness of the truth.[6] The principal argument of this essay is that the pursuit of excellence, like the mind's original constitution, discloses humanity's ontological orientation toward the highest and most supreme good, namely, the perfect apprehension of God in heaven (cf. 1 Cor. 13:12).

Stewardship of Talents: The Intellectual Divide between Religious Leaders and Entrepreneurs

The time has come for religious institutions and leaders to treat entrepreneurship as a worthy vocation, indeed, as a sacred calling. All lay people have a special role to play in the economy of salvation, sharing in the task of furthering the faith by using their talents in complementary ways. Every person created in the image of God has been given certain natural abilities that God desires to be cultivated and treated as good gifts. If the gift happens to be an inclination for business, stock trading, or investment banking, the religious community should not condemn the person merely on account of his or her profession.

In response to my writings in a variety of business journals, people of a particular profile contact me. On one occasion a gentleman called to let me know that he had just finished reading an article of mine in Forbes. It was, as he explained, both a shocking and emotional experience—shocking, because in all of his Roman Catholic school education and regular church attendance, he had never before heard a priest speak insightfully of the responsibilities, tensions, and risks inherent in running a business. Was there, he wondered, no spiritual component at all in what occupied so much of his life? In reading the article, he felt affirmed—for the first time—by a religious leader at the point in his life where he spent most of his time and effort: in the world of work.

This man represents many others whose stories are too numerous to recount here. Very often, they are relatively successful individuals with deep moral and religious convictions. However, each experiences a moral tension, not because what he or she does is somehow wrong, but because religious leadership has usually failed to grasp the dynamics of his or her vocation and thus provide relevant moral guidance and affirmation.

These people represent a variety of Christian traditions, and they all express a sense of being disenfranchised and alienated from their Churches. Religious leaders generally display very little understanding of the entrepreneurial vocation, of what it requires, and of what it contributes to society. Unfortunately, ignorance of the facts has not kept them from moralizing on economic matters and causing great harm to the spiritual development of business people. In particular, I recall one man, a self-described conservative Christian, saying that he no longer attended church services because he refused to sit in the pew with his family and, in effect, be chastised for his business acumen. How many critical sermons can a small-business owner or investment banker hear before he or she loses heart and decides to sleep in on the Sabbath?

Michael Novak relates another experience demonstrating the almost impenetrable resistance that some clergy exhibit to conceding the moral potential of market liberalism. His experience occurred at a conference on economics in which several Latin American priests were participating. The conference went on for several days, during which a persuasive case was made for how the free economy is capable of lifting the poor from poverty through the productive means of the market. The priests remained silent until the final day of the conference, and Novak offers an interesting account of what happened next:

> At the last session of what had been a happy seminar, one of the priests arose to say that his colleagues had assembled the night before and asked him to make a statement on their behalf. "We have," he said, "greatly enjoyed this week. We have learned a great deal. We see very well that capitalism is the most effective means of producing wealth, and even that it distributes wealth more broadly and more evenly than the economic systems we see in Latin America. But we still think that capitalism is an immoral system."[7]

Why does this state of affairs exist? Why is it so common that business people hear nothing better from a religious leader than something akin to, "Well, the way to redeem yourself is to give us your money"? Why is it that many of those who form the moral conscience of our world simply do not grasp either the moral foundation or basic principles of the market?

An obvious reason for this ignorance is the astonishing lack of any economics training in virtually all seminaries. It is rare to find a single seminary course explaining fundamental economic principles, the complicated world of stock trading, or micro-economic dynamics. Historically, in most social ethics courses, seminarians were accustomed to hearing the empty slogans of liberation-theology proponents who believed that developed nations exploit less-developed nations, thus keeping them in a perpetual state of poverty.[8] Generally, these arguments were put forth by theologians who had little grasp of economics.

The Practical Divide between Religious Leaders and Entrepreneurs

In addition to an intellectual or academic gap, there is frequently a kind of practical divide between religious leaders and entre-preneurs in their understanding of market operations. This is because the two groups tend to operate from different world-views and employ different models in their daily operations. Notice how these differences are typically manifested. On Sunday morning a collection basket is passed in most churches. On Monday the bills are paid, acts of charity attended to, and levies paid to denominational headquarters. However, when the collection regularly comes up short, making it difficult to pay the bills, most ministers will preach a sermon on the responsi-bility of stewardship. In the minds of many clergy, economic decisions resemble dividing up a pie into equal slices. In this view, wealth is seen as a static entity, which means that for someone with a small sliver to increase his or her share of the pie, someone else must necessarily receive a somewhat smaller piece. The "moral solution" that springs from this economic model is the redistribution of wealth, what might be called a "Robin Hood" morality.

Entrepreneurs operate from a very different understanding of money and wealth. They speak of "making" money, not of "collecting" it; of producing wealth, not of redistributing it. Entrepreneurs must consider the needs, wants, and desires of consumers, because the only way to meet their own needs peacefully—without relying on charity—is to offer something of value in exchange. These people, then, view the world of money as dynamic. In referring to the free market as dynamic, however, it is easy to get the impression that we are describing a place or an object. However, the market is actually a process—a series of choices made by independently acting persons who themselves place monetary values on goods and services. This process of assigning subjectively determined values is responsible for producing the "wealth of nations," a phrase that is typically associated with the title of Adam Smith's classic eighteenth-century work[9] but was actually first employed in the Book of Isaiah (60:5).[10] The creative view of economics taken by business people is also illustrated in Scripture.

Unfortunately, the preceding argument may be misconstrued as urging that religion adopt a bottom-line, profit-and-loss mentality with regard to its mission, but this would be a grave distortion. I agree that there is a significant place for the sharing of wealth and resources within Christian practice—indeed, a mandatory place. With their transcendent vision, communities of faith recognize that some matters cannot be placed within the limited calculus of economic exchange or evaluated solely in terms of money. It is equally true, however, that to maintain credibility in the world of business and finance, clergy must first understand the inner workings of the market economy, for only then will such moral guidance be helpful.

But there is another, if somewhat misleading, factor that contributes to the hostility toward capitalism that one frequently encounters in religious circles. Many religious leaders spend a great portion of their lives personally confronting the wretchedness of poverty. Poverty saddens and angers us, and we want to put an end to it. This sentiment is entirely proper, not to mention morally incumbent upon Christians. However, a problem develops when this sentiment is combined with the economic ignorance described above. When this happens, the just cry against poverty is converted into an illegitimate rage against wealth as such, as though the latter created the former. While this reaction is understandable, it is nevertheless ill-informed and can lead to overreactions. Persons who react in this way fail to acknowledge that the amelioration of poverty will be achieved only by producing wealth and protecting a free economy.

The Propriety of Moral Outrage

There is understandable moral resistance to the image of successful business enterprise if one presumes that the engine of such activity is animated by greed, acquisitiveness, selfishness, or pride. The issue is not that some entrepreneurs are greedy or proud but whether these character flaws are the *norm* for successful practitioners of enterprise. The intent here is not to gloss over the fact that there are serious temptations associated with wealth and success but to come to a more balanced assessment of the moral character of entrepreneurs.

For some reason, moral critics often focus on the personal gains of entrepreneurs—as if wealth itself is somehow unjust—but lose sight of the many personal risks shouldered by these individuals. Long before entrepreneurs see a return on their idea or investment, they must surrender their time and property to an unknown fate. They pay out wages even before they know whether their forecast has been accurate. They have no assurance of profit. When investments do return a profit, much of it is usually reinvested (and some of it goes to charities and religious institutions). Sometimes entrepreneurs make errors of judgment and miscalculations, and the business suffers financial loss. The nature of the vocation is such that entrepreneurs themselves must accept responsibility for their losses without shifting the burden onto the public. For the person with a true vocation to be an economic agent of change, he or she must remain vigilant, for economic conditions are always changing.

When an economic risk fails, religious professionals should consider if it is not better to encourage than to condemn. Or should economic losses suffered by capitalists be viewed as their just deserts? Why not make such occasions opportunities to extend sympathy or pastoral care instead? *Whether they win or lose, by putting themselves and their property on the line, entrepreneurs make the future a little more secure for the rest of us.*

What is unique about the institution of entrepreneurship is that it requires no third-party intervention either to establish or to maintain it. It requires no governmental program or governmental manuals. It does not require low-interest loans, special tax treatment, or public subsidies. It does not even require specialized education or a prestigious degree. Entrepreneurship is an institution that develops organically from human intelligence situated in the context of the natural order of liberty. Those with the talent, calling, and aptitude for economic creativity are compelled to enter the entrepreneurial vocation for the purpose of producing goods and services and providing jobs.

Truly, the gifts that entrepreneurs offer society at large are beyond anything either they or others can fully comprehend. *Entrepreneurs are the source of more social and spiritual good than is generally recognized.* This fact, however, does not gainsay a pastor's proper role of spiritual direction, addressing not only moral failures but also misplaced priorities, neglect of family, and inattention to spiritual development due to overwork. Clergy must remind everyone of the seriousness of sin and call them to virtue, which means they must likewise challenge entrepreneurs when they go astray. To be authentic, this spiritual direction must be grounded in an understanding of what Judaism and Christianity have traditionally understood as sin, not in some politically correct economic ideology masquerading as moral theology.

This is a difficult transition for many religious leaders to make, especially because their inherited moral framework for understanding economic productivity was developed in a pre-capitalist world. It is an arduous undertaking to translate and apply pre-modern Christian social teaching to the dynamic environment of a modern, post-agrarian, post-industrial, and now, post-Communist world. It is especially difficult because, while human nature does not change, the socio-economic context in which human nature exists is radically different from those cultures and societies where the principles of moral theology were first developed.[11]

Entrepreneurs and Economists: Family Squabble or Sibling Rivalry?

Economic theory has long had difficulty coming to terms with the nature of entrepreneurship, probably because it does not fit well into the econometric equations and graphs that depict the economy as a large machine. Entrepreneur-ship is too human an endeavor to be understood by science alone. That is where religion can be helpful in reconciling such people to the life of faith. Religious leaders must seek to understand entrepreneurs and encourage them to use their gifts within the context of faith. Of course, with wealth comes responsibility, and Pope John Paul II insists that even the decision to invest has an inescapable moral dimension.[12] Yet, entrepreneurs, by taking risks, serving the public, and expanding the economic pie for everyone, can be counted among the greatest men and women of faith in the Church.

Anti-Capitalist Capitalists

Even more puzzling than the anti-capitalist bias among the clergy is the bias found among capitalists themselves. In misguided attempts to achieve a high level of "social responsibility" for their companies, some business leaders have succumbed to false views of the marketplace. While creating wealth for society through their successful businesses, they simultaneously support causes antithetical to economic growth, free enterprise, and human liberty. Why does the rhetoric of "corporate social responsibility" seem to have such an anti-capitalistic bias? In the mid-1990s it became increasingly apparent that otherwise successful chief executive officers were using their corporations to fund politically interventionist causes under the rubric of corporate social responsibility. This could be seen particularly in the cases of Patagonia, Ben and Jerry's ice cream, and The Body Shop cosmetics chain.

Yvon Chouinard is the founder of Patagonia, a successful producer of functional outdoor sports clothing. Chouinard told the *Los Angeles Times* that he can "sit down one-on-one with the president of any company, anytime, anywhere, and convince [him or her] that growth is evil." His words, in fact, match his actions. In 1991 the company sent a letter to its dealers, announcing that it was "curtailing domestic growth" for economic and moral reasons. "We've taken a public stand in favor of more rational consumption in order to benefit the environment," the statement read. But, as *Los Angeles Times* reporter Kenneth Bodenstein relates, the situation in 1991 was quite different from Chouinard's public statements. It turns out that Patagonia had not "curtailed domestic growth" to maintain a high standard of social responsibility. "The company actually fired thirty percent of its staff, not because [it] was in deep financial trouble but because Yvon Chouinard's personal wealth was threatened." Interestingly, in Bodenstein's appraisal, Patagonia's situation resulted from ill-informed economic decisions such as Choui-nard having "surrounded himself with managers with too little experience."[13]

Patagonia is, indeed, an unusual company. Chouinard donates one percent of Patagonia's total sales to environmental groups, including Earth First, an organization that gained notoriety for sabotaging logging machinery and infringing on private property rights. Patagonia also supports Planned Parenthood on the grounds that an increase in population threatens the future well-being of the planet. Chouinard desires his company to be a shining moral example to the corporate world. "If we can take the radical end of it and show it is working for us, the more conservative companies will take that first step. And one day they will become good businesses, too," he quips.

Ice cream entrepreneurs Ben Cohen and Jerry Greenfield, of Ben and Jerry's fame, though enormously successful as entrepreneurs, promote burdensome environmental controls and advocate giving welfare recipients broader rights to the public purse. Cohen and Greenfield have been leaders in the movement to restrict the production of bovine growth hormone, a drug that, when injected into cows, can increase milk output by up to fifteen percent. They oppose the drug on economic grounds because they believe that it poses a threat to small-scale dairy farmers. However, the hormone, which was approved by the United States Food and Drug Administra-tion on August 4, 1997, would also push down the price of milk, something that would be particularly helpful to poor families, if not to ice cream producers.

The Body Shop, the cosmetics chain with a naturalist bent, has been a vociferous supporter of animal rights and other left-wing causes. The company's founder and managing director, Anita Roddick, is a self-appointed preacher to the corporate world, chiding business people who are not "doing their share." "I am not talking about people who are just scraping up a living.... I am talking about people who have huge, huge profits," she told the *Arizona Republic*. "You know, these CEOS with compensation packages bigger than the GNPS of some African countries."[14]

There are countless companies run by former 1960s-style radicals who try to reconcile their business success with the values of their youth. Everyone, business people included, has a right to advocate a chosen cause, as all customers have the right not to fund their causes by boycotting their products. But the pattern of these entrepreneurs displays an internal incoherence and suggests an attempt to do penance for capitalist "sins," which are not really sins at all.

These penitent capitalists castigate businesses that do not give enough back to society. A misplaced sense of guilt has clouded their understanding of how their own businesses do good for society, independently of social activism. Patagonia produces top-quality sporting goods. Ben and Jerry's serves up superior ice cream. The Body Shop sells inexpensive, all-natural cosmetics. Each of these companies brings satisfaction to millions and provides good products as well as jobs and investment opportunities. Their market success does not—and should not—need to be justified by support of anti-market causes.

The cynic might suggest that such postures are little more than marketing gimmicks. Socially aware chief executive officers such as Chouinard, Cohen, Greenfield, and Roddick have packaged 1960s idealism and are selling it for profit. When you buy a pint of Ben and Jerry's Rain Forest Crunch ice cream, you can feel good about helping save what used to be called "the jungle." The left-wing political slogans that adorn The Body Shop franchises are part of the image of cosmetics for the young and "socially aware." Such companies as Patagonia, Ben and Jerry's, and the Body Shop sell a mingled sense of moral superiority. These business people, using politically correct advertising slogans, can believe that despite their material success, they are giving something back to the world. Yet their "social responsibility" campaigns often become an irresponsible recipe for economic ruin.

These companies, and others like them, certainly profit from their association with left-wing causes. Meanwhile, taxpayers suffer from the advocacy of strict environmental controls, restrictions on FDA-approved growth hormones, and permissive attitudes toward sexual conduct. And would-be entrepreneurs are inhibited by new environmental regulations and welfare programs. We may commend business when it supports charities that lift people out of poverty, or purchases land to be preserved, or explores cures for diseases; *legitimate causes do not impede the market or push for more ill-conceived governmental action to solve social problems.* However, capitalism does not need more guilt-ridden leftists publicly flogging themselves and others for making money. Rather, capitalism needs more business people who understand that their greatest contribution lies in making profits, expanding jobs, boosting investment, increasing prosperity—and doing so in a way that promotes a wholesome, stable, and virtuous culture. *The proper moral response to capitalist success is both praise for the Creator who has provided the material world as a gift for all and also support of the economic system that allows prosperity to flourish.* Rather than doing needless penance, entrepreneurs such as Chouinard, Cohen, Greenfield, and Roddick should study fundamental economic theory—not to mention basic moral theology.

Dominion Theology and Economic Ideology

So far, we have discussed the aberrant "wealth-is-evil" branch of theological thinking held by so many clergy and even some entrepreneurs. However, there is a second branch that stems from the same root but takes an opposite approach. This is seen in what is called dominion theology or *Christian reconstruction.*[15] In response to liberation theology and the evangelical left, dominion theologians insist not only that the Bible provides the blueprint for structuring every aspect of society but also that as Christians attain a fuller understanding of the Bible, they will progressively take dominion over society, which will eventually usher in the kingdom of God. According to this theory, Christians will achieve global dominion, therefore, by voluntarily adopting the economic and sociological blueprint outlined in Scripture. Theonomist Gary North argues that applying these principles over time will naturally make Christians affluent, enabling them to procreate effectively and prolifically.[16] Thus, as Christians become increasingly affluent, numerous, and powerful, they will assume control of society. There is a natural correlation, it seems, between the theonomist's rationalization of personal affluence and the so-called prosperity gospel popular in Neo-Pentecostalism. Proponents of the prosperity gospel, also known as the health-and-wealth gospel, believe that God wants all Christians to be both healthy and wealthy and that there are certain "laws of prosperity" that, when applied correctly, inevitably produce these results.[17] Those who hold this view not only consider wealth as a sign of God's blessing but also intimate that economic hardship is a result of sin. Craig Gay pinpoints how dominion theology and the prosperity gospel coalesce:

> In a sense, then, dominion theology takes [the health and wealth] position several steps further, suggesting that individual aspirations to wealth fit into an eschatological framework that further legitimates them. From the perspective of Christian reconstructionism, the failure of Christians to become wealthy is not simply an indication of a lack of faith but actually postpones the coming of the kingdom of God.[18]

While dominion theologians correctly affirm the importance of free-market economics, they also espouse an unbalanced and unbiblical view of the cultural mandate, creation theology, eschatology, and the reign of Christ. Such theological excesses might be curbed if partisans of both the left and the right were to consult (more frequently) the history of Christian thought for guidance in these matters.

Entrepreneurship as a Spiritual Vocation

Implicitly, and, at times, explicitly, faithful parishioners assume that the only real calling is to some kind of full-time Church work. In this view, lay people do not really have a vocation, though they do the best they can, given the circumstances. In 1891, canon law offered a simple but devastating definition of the lay person: "Lay: not clerical."[19] Since then, especially under the influence of the Second Vatican Council, a far more positive view has emerged, one that plumbs the depths of God's missionary objectives both inside and outside of the church.[20]

Looking at the gift of business acumen in an alternative way, however, enables us to grasp its spiritual and moral potential. An entrepreneur is someone who connects capital, labor, and material factors in order to produce a good or service. Michael Novak has argued that the entrepreneur's creativity is akin to God's creative activity in the first chapter of Genesis. In this sense, the entrepreneur participates in the original cultural mandate, given by God to Adam and Eve, to subdue the earth.[21] The entrepreneurial vocation is a sacred call similar to that of being a parent, even if it is not quite as sublime.

For several years, I have participated in programs designed to teach seminarians the importance of the free economy and the responsibilities of the entrepreneur. For many of these students, the ideas presented lead to eye-opening experiences. Students discover that the free-market system is about creating wealth, about finding more effcient ways of serving others, and about providing people with jobs and investment opportunities. They discover that the chasm separating prosperity and morality is no longer insuperable.

In these seminars, I often mention George Gilder's extraordinary book *Wealth and Poverty*.[22] It can even be argued, I think, that Gilder is something of an intellectual entrepreneur. It is *Wealth and Poverty* that has been credited with being the intellectual force behind the 1980s' supply-side revolution, which forced economists and policy makers to consider for the first time how governmental policy, especially in the area of taxation, affects human choices. The popularity of this book illustrates well how someone outside academia can exert tremendous influence on American economic life. In my view, however, Gilder accomplished something much more important by insisting that *entrepreneurship is a morally legitimate profession*.

Gilder regards entrepreneurs as among the most misunderstood and underappreciated groups in society. As visionaries with practical instincts, entrepreneurs combine classical and Christian virtues to advance their own interests and those of society. Gilder thinks it is a mistake to associate capitalism with greed—an association with altruism would be far more accurate.[23] When people accept the challenge of an entrepreneurial vocation, they have implicitly decided to meet the needs of others through the goods or services they produce. If the entrepreneur's investments are to return a profit, the entrepreneur must be "other-directed." *Ultimately, business persons in a market economy simply cannot be both self-centered and successful.*[24]

The final chapter of *Wealth and Poverty* is perhaps the least read but most crucial of the entire book. Here Gilder presents the theory that entrepreneurship is an act of faith, an inescapably religious act.[25] By fusing traditional Christian morality with a celebration of growth and change, he helps us discern how knowledge and discovery are essential elements of enterprise.

Long before the publication of Gilder's Wealth and Poverty, an entire school of economics had grown up around Joseph Schumpeter's insight into entrepreneurship. According to

Schumpeter, it was entrepreneurship—more than any other economic institution—that prevented economic and technological torpor from retarding economic growth. He thought that the function of entrepreneurs is

> to reform or revolutionize the pattern of production by exploiting an invention or, more generally, an untried technological possibility for producing a new commodity or producing an old one in a new way, by opening up a new source of supply of materials or a new outlet for products, by reorganizing an industry and so on.[26]

Entrepreneurs, as agents of change, encourage the economy to adjust to population increases, resource shifts, and changes in consumer needs and desires. Without entrepreneurs, we would face a static economic world not unlike the stagnant economic swamps that socialism brought about in central Europe.

The economic analysis that has its roots in Schumpeter's work taught that entrepreneurs are *impresarios*, visionaries who organize numerous factors, take risks, and combine resources to create something greater than the sum of its parts.[27] Entrepreneurs drive the economy forward by anticipating the wishes of the public and creating new ways of organizing resources. In short, they are men and women who create jobs, discover and apply new cures, bring food to those in need, and help dreams become realities.

The Biblical Case for Entrepreneurship

Those who consider the entrepreneurial vocation a necessary evil, who view profits with open hostility, should realize that Scripture lends ample support to entrepreneurial activity. The Bible teaches us eternal truths but also provides surprisingly practical lessons for worldly affairs. In Matthew 25:14–30, we find Jesus' parable of the talents. As with all parables, its meaning is multi-layered. Its eternal meaning relates to how we use

God's gift of grace. With regard to the material world, it is a story about capital, investment, entrepreneurship, and the proper use of economic resources. It is a direct rebuttal to those who insist that business success and Christian living are contradictory. What follows is the text of this parable (NRSV) with commentary that applies principles taken from the parable to the entrepreneurial vocation.

> For it is as if a man, going on a journey, summoned his slaves and entrusted his property to them; to one he gave five talents; to another, two; to another, one, to each according to his ability. Then he went away. The one who had received the five talents went off at once and traded with them, and made five more talents. In the same way, the one who had the two talents made two more talents. But the one who had received the one talent went off and dug a hole in the ground and hid his master's money. After a long time, the master of those slaves came and settled accounts with them. Then the one who had received the five talents came forward, bringing five more talents, saying, "Master, you handed over to me five talents; see, I have made five more talents." His master said to him, "Well done, good and trustworthy slave; you have been trustworthy in a few things, I will put you in charge of many things; enter into the joy of your master." And the one with two talents also came forward, saying, "Master, you handed over to me two talents; see, I have made two more talents." His master said to him, "Well done, good and trustworthy slave; you have been trustworthy in a few things, I will put you in charge of many things; enter into the joy of your master." Then the one who had received the one talent also came forward, saying, "Master, I knew that you were a harsh man, reaping where you did not sow, and gathering where you did not scatter seed; so I was afraid, and I went and hid your talent in the ground. Here you have what is yours." But his master replied,

23

"You wicked and lazy slave! You knew, did you, that I reap where I did not sow, and gather where I did not scatter? Then you ought to have invested my money with the bankers, and on my return I would have received what was my own with interest. So take the talent from him, and give it to the one with the ten talents. For to all those who have, more will be given, and they will have an abundance; but from those who have nothing, even what they have will be taken away. As for this worthless slave, throw him into the outer darkness, where there will be weeping and gnashing of teeth." (Matt. 25:14–30, NRSV)

This is a story that many religious leaders do not often apply to real life. When people think of Jesus' parables, the parable of the talents is not usually the first to come to mind. Perhaps this is because most religious leaders hold to an ethic where profit is suspect and entrepreneurship is frowned upon. Yet the preceding story relays an immediately apparent ethical meaning, not to mention even deeper lessons for economic accountability and proper stewardship.

The word *talent* in this parable has two meanings. First, it is a monetary unit, perhaps even the largest denomination of Jesus' time. The editors of the *New Bible Commentary* agree that a talent was a very large sum of money; in modern terms, it would have been equivalent to several thousand dollars.[28] So, we know that the amount given to each servant was considerable. Second, more broadly interpreted, the word *talent* refers to all of the various gifts God has given us to cultivate and multiply. This definition embraces all gifts, including our natural abilities and resources as well as our health, education, possessions, money, and opportunities.

I do not pretend to build an entire ethic for capitalism from this parable. To do so would be to commit an egregious exegetical and historical error, similar to those committed by liberation and dominion theologians. Yet, *one of the simplest lessons from this parable has to do with how we use our God-given capacities and resources.* This, I contend, must be part of an ethic that guides economic activity and decision-making in the marketplace. On one level, in the same way the master expected productive activity from his servants, God wants us to use our talents toward constructive ends. We see here that in setting off on his journey, the master allows his servants to decide upon the best manner of investment. In this regard, they have full liberty. In fact, the master does not even command them to invest profitably; instead, he merely assumes their goodwill and interest in his property. Given this implicit trust, it is easier to understand the master's eventual disgust with the unprofitable servant. It is not so much his lack of productivity that offends the master as the underlying attitude he exhibits toward the master and his property. One can imagine the servant's reasoning: "I'll just get by; I'll put this talent out of sight so that I don't have to deal with it, monitor it, or be accountable for it." One biblical scholar, Leopold Fonck, observes, "It is not the misuse only of the gifts received which renders the recipient guilty in the sight of God, but the non-use also."[29] The master invited each of the diligent servants to rejoice in his own joy, once they had shown themselves to be productive. They were handsomely rewarded; indeed, the master gave the lazy servant's single talent to the one who had been given ten.

The parable of the talents, however, presupposes a local understanding of the proper stewardship of money. According to rabbinical law, burying was regarded as the best security against theft. If a person entrusted with money buried it as soon as he took possession of it, he would be free from liability, should anything happen to it. For money merely tied up in a cloth, the opposite was true. In this case, the person was responsible to cover any loss incurred due to the irresponsible nature of the deposit.[30] Yet, in the parable of the talents, the master encourages reasonable risk-taking. He considers the act of burying the talent—and thus breaking even—to be foolish, because he believes capital should earn a reasonable rate of return. In this understanding, time is money (another way of discussing interest).

A second critical lesson from the parable is this: *It is not immoral to profit from our resources, wit, and labor.* Though writing for an entirely different audience and context, Austrian economist Israel Kirzner employs the concept of entrepreneurial alertness to show the significance of cultivating one's natural ability, time, and resources. Building on the work of Ludwig von Mises, Kirzner acknowledges that by seeking new opportunities and engaging in goal-directed activity, entrepreneurs strive "to pursue goals efficiently, once ends and means are clearly identified, but also with the drive and alertness needed to identify which ends to strive for and which means are available."[31] Without overstating the similarity between Kirzner's concept and the parable of the talents, there seems to be a natural connection between the discovery of entrepreneurial opportunities and the master's (the Lord's) admonition in Matthew 25 to be watchful of his return and to be caretakers of his property. Thus, with respect to profit, the only alternative is loss, which, in the case of the third servant, constitutes poor stewardship.[32] However, the voluntary surrender of wealth, such as in almsgiving or in its more radical form of renouncing the right to ownership of property (as in the traditional vow of poverty taken by members of certain religious orders),[33] should not be confused with economic loss. In the former case, a legitimate good is foregone in exchange for another to which one has been uniquely called. In the latter case, to fail deliberately in an economic endeavor, or to do so as a result of sloth, is to show disrespect for God's gift and for one's responsibility as a steward.

Nevertheless, we must distinguish properly between the moral obligations to be economically creative and productive, on the one hand, and to employ one's talents and resources prudently and magnanimously, on the other. It is clear from our discussion of the parable of the talents and the cultural mandate in Genesis 1 that in subduing the earth, people need to be attentive to the possibilities for change, development, and investment. Furthermore, because humans are created in the image of God and have been endowed with reason and free will, human actions necessarily involve a creative dimension. Thus, in the case of the third servant who placed his single talent into the ground, it was the non-use of his ability to remain alert to future possibilities—which precluded any productive return on the master's money—that led to his being severely chastised.

There is, perhaps, no clearer illustration of employing one's talents and resources prudently for the good of all than the monks of the medieval Cistercian monasteries. Insofar as monasteries were ruled by a religious constitution that divided each monk's day into segments devoted to prayer, contemplation, worship, and work, the amount of time available to spend on productive activities was tightly regulated. This constraint, along with the typical monastic emphasis on self-sufficiency, motivated monasteries to develop more efficient farm-production techniques, which provided a natural incentive to embrace technological development. In addition to the early and frequent use of mills, Cistercian monks also experimented with plants, soils, and breeding stocks, thus enabling them to use their God-given creativity wisely and productively in order to accumulate money for the monastery and to aid the poor.[34]

Economics shows that the rate of return (profit) on capital over the long run is likely to equal the interest rate. The rate of interest, in turn, is the payment given for putting off present consumption for future consumption (sometimes called the rate of time preference). For the master in Jesus' parable, it was not enough merely to recover the original value of the talent; rather, he expected the servant to increase its value through participation in the economy. Even a minimal level of participation, such as keeping money in an interest-bearing account, would have yielded a small rate of return on the master's capital. Burying capital in the ground sacrifices even that minimal amount of return, which was what incensed the master about his servant's indolence.

In the book of Genesis, we read that God gave the earth with all its resources to Adam and Eve. Adam was to mix his labor with the raw material of creation to produce usable goods for his family.[35] Similarly, the master in the parable of the talents expected his servants to use the resources at their disposal to increase the value of his holdings. Rather than passively preserve what they had been given, the two faithful servants invested the money, but the master was justly angered at the timidity of the servant who had received one talent. Through this parable, God commands us to use our talents productively. Through this parable, we are exhorted to work, be creative, and reject idleness.

Throughout history, people have endeavored to construct institutions that ensure security and minimize risk—much as the failed servant tried to do with the master's money. Such efforts range from the Greco-Roman welfare States, to the Luddite communes of the 1960s, to full-scale Soviet totalitarianism. From time to time, these efforts have been embraced as "Christian" solutions to future insecurities. Yet, uncertainty is not just a hazard to be avoided; it can be an opportunity to glorify God through wise use of his gifts. In the parable of the talents, courage in the face of an unknown future was generously rewarded in the case of the first servant, who had been entrusted with the most. He used the five talents to acquire five more. It would have been safer for him to deposit the money in a bank and receive a nominal interest rate. For taking reasonable risks and displaying entrepreneurial acumen, he was allowed to retain his original allotment as well as his new earnings. Furthermore, he was even invited to rejoice with the master.

The lazy servant could have avoided his dismal fate by demonstrating more entrepreneurial initiative. If he had made an effort to increase his master's holdings but failed in the process, he may not have been judged so harshly.

The parable of the talents implies a moral obligation to confront uncertainty in an enterprising way. There is no more apt example of such an individual than that of the entrepreneur. Entrepreneurs look to the future with courage and a sense of opportunity. In creating new enterprises, they open up new options for people with regard to earning a wage and developing their skills. But none of what has been argued should be taken to imply that the entrepreneur, because of the importance that he or she holds for society, should be exempted from spiritual accountability. Immoral behavior can be found among entrepreneurs no less often than among any other group of sinful human beings. However, *it is important neither to canonize poverty nor to demonize economic success.*

No doubt, in the pursuit of their vocation, business leaders will be tempted in many ways. Sometimes the temptation will be thinking that the humdrum world of business and finance is spiritually insignificant and that the bottom line is paramount. In such moments, entrepreneurs must reflect anew on the twenty-fifth chapter of Matthew's gospel and grasp the fact that God has entrusted them with their talents and that he expects entrepreneurs to be industrious, generous, and innovative with them. And if they will be faithful to this calling, they may hope to hear the words spoken by the Master to those first servants: "Well done, thou good and faithful servant. Thou hast been faithful over a few things; I will make thee ruler over many things. Enter thou into the joy of thy Lord." (Matt. 25:21, KJV)

Notes

1. Charles Dickens, *Hard Times for These Times* (London: Oxford University Press, 1955 [1854]); *Dealings with the Firm of Dombey and Son, Wholesale, Retail, and for Exportation* (London: Oxford University Press, 1964 [1847–1848]).

2. Sinclair Lewis, *Babbitt* (New York: Harcourt, Brace, and Company, 1922).

3. For a fuller description of how businesspeople have been depicted in literature, see Michael J. McTague, *The Businessman in Literature: Dante to Melville* (New York: Philosophical Library, 1979).

4. Ibid., 63–71.

5. The quintessential historical representative of this position would be Bernard Mandeville, who thought that economic prosperity resulted from the actions of self-seeking and amoral individuals. He argued that to achieve economic success, people must be liberated from the restraints of conventional morality. This relegated the prescriptions of business ethics to the status of useful fictions created to maintain order and ensure predictable results. *The Fable of*

the Bees, vol. 1, ed. F. B. Kaye (London: Oxford University Press, 1924 [1705]), 46. For a criticism of Mandeville and his contemporary followers, see Norman P. Barry, *Anglo-American Capitalism and the Ethics of Business* (Wellington, New Zealand: New Zealand Business Roundtable, 1999), 8–16; also cf., Norman P. Barry, *The Morality of Business Enterprise* (Aberdeen: Aberdeen University Press, 1991), 3–6.

6. John Paul II, *Crossing the Threshold of Hope*, ed. Vittorio Messori (New York: Alfred A. Knopf, 1994), 32–36; Encyclical Letter *Fides et Ratio* (September 14, 1998), nos. 4–5, 27.

7. Michael Novak, *This Hemisphere of Liberty: A Philosophy of the Americas* (Washington, D.C.: AEI Press, 1990), 38.

8. According to Gregory Baum, then professor of theology and religious studies at Saint Michael's College, University of Toronto, "… the economic dependence of the Latin American countries on the system of corporate capitalism, with its center in the North Atlantic community and more especially in the United States, has not only led to the impoverishment of the mass of the population in the city and country but also has affected the cultural and educational institutions and through them the consciousness of the people in general." *The Social Imperative: Essays on the Critical Issues That Confront the Christian Churches* (New York: Paulist Press, 1979), 10. Or, as Northwestern University professor Rosemary Ruether writes: "… it is only in Latin America that the real theology of liberation can be written, whereas Europeans and North Americans, who remain encompassed by their own status as beneficiaries of oppressive power, can only comment upon this theology from outside." *Liberation Theology: Human Hope Confronts Christian History and American Power* (New York: Paulist Press, 1972), 181. For a cogent critique of these approaches, see Michael Novak, *Will It Liberate? Questions About Liberation Theology* (New York: Paulist Press, 1986).

9. Adam Smith, *An Inquiry into the Nature and Causes of the Wealth of Nations*, ed. R. H. Campbell and A. S. Skinner (Oxford: Oxford University Press, 1976 [1776]).

10. The text of the verse reads (NRSV):
> Then you shall see and be radiant;
> > Your heart shall thrill and rejoice,
> because the abundance of the sea shall be brought to you,
> > the wealth of the nations shall come to you.

11. In the two years preceding his reception into the Roman Catholic Church (1843–1845), John Henry Cardinal Newman wrote his now-famous work, *An Essay on the Development of Christian Doctrine* (London: J. Toovey, 1845). Unfortunately, then as now, it is all too common that well-meaning and faithful Roman Catholics associate a growing Christian self-understanding and maturity in the area of doctrine and morals with a relativist worldview. It is true that some theologians are in jeopardy of slipping into relativism; however, to argue, as some do, that any doctrinal emendation will necessarily lead to relativism is false. In the case of Cardinal Newman, the main task of his essay was to examine the principal differences between doctrinal corruption and doctrinal development. In the essay, he insists that a true and fertile idea is endowed with a certain vital and assimilative energy of its own, which, without experiencing substantive change, attains a more complete expression as it encounters new aspects of truth or collides with new errors over time. Thus, Cardinal Newman employs an organic metaphor to describe how doctrinal ideas develop over the course of time through the Church's new experiences, discoveries, and revelations. To bolster his argument, he provides a series of tests for distinguishing true development from corruption, the chief of which are the preservation of type and the continuity of principles. It is important to grasp, therefore, that the essence of the doctrine—*both in its earlier and later forms*—was contained in the original revelation given to the church by Christ and the apostles, and guaranteed by its Magisterium.

12. John Paul II, Encyclical Letter *Centesimus Annus* (May 1, 1991), nos. 29, 32.

13. Kenneth Bodenstein, "Pure Profit: For Small Companies That Stress Social Values As Much As the Bottom Line, Growing Up Hasn't Been an Easy Task," *Los Angeles Times Magazine* (February 5, 1995): 4.

14. Jodie Snyder, "Social Awareness: Corporate America Cultivates Conscience," *Arizona Republic* (May 12, 1994): 6.

15. The principal representatives of dominion theology are: Gary North, Rousas J. Rushdoony, Greg Bahnsen, David Chilton, Rodney Clapp, and Gary DeMar.

16. Gary North, *Liberating Planet Earth: An Introduction to Biblical Blueprints* (Fort Worth: Dominion Press, 1987), 81.

17. See Bruce Barton, *The Health and Wealth Gospel* (Downers Grove, Ill.: InterVarsity Press, 1987).

18. Craig M. Gay, *With Liberty and Justice for Whom? The Recent Evangelical Debate Over Capitalism* (Grand Rapids: Eerdmans, 1991), 103, ftn. 191. For an incisive exposition and critique of dominion theology, see pages 101–9.

19. See Yves Congar, O.P., "The Laity," in *Vatican II: An Interfaith Appraisal* (Notre Dame: University of Notre Dame Press, 1966), 240.

20. *In Gaudium et Spes*, the Second Vatican Council promulgates a much more positive understanding of the role of the laity. In paragraph 43, the Council states:

> Let Christians follow the example of Christ, who worked as a craftsman; let them be proud of the opportunity to carry out their earthly activity in such a way as to integrate human, domestic, professional, scientific, and technical enterprises with religious values, under whose supreme direction all things are ordered to the glory of God.
>
> It is to the laity, though not exclusively to them, that secular duties and activity properly belong. When, therefore, as citizens of the world, they are engaged in any activity either individually or collectively, they will not be satisfied with meeting the minimum legal requirements but will strive to become truly proficient in that sphere.... It is to their task to cultivate a properly informed conscience and to impress the divine law on the affairs of the earthly city. For guidance and spiritual strength let them turn to the clergy but let them realize that their pastors will not always be so expert as to have a ready answer to every problem (even every grave problem) that

arises; this is not the role of the clergy: It is, rather, up to the laymen to shoulder their responsibilities under the guidance of Christian wisdom and with eager attention to the teaching authority of the Church....

The laity are called to participate actively in the whole life of the Church; not only are they to animate the world with the spirit of Christianity, but they are to be witnesses to Christ in all circumstances and at the very heart of the community of mankind.

21. Michael Novak, *The Spirit of Democratic Capitalism* (New York: Simon and Schuster, 1982), 98.

22. George Gilder, *Wealth and Poverty*, rev. ed. (San Francisco: ICS Press, 1993).

23. Ibid., 21, 24.

24. Ibid., 28.

25. Ibid., 276–80.

26. Joseph A. Schumpeter, *Capitalism, Socialism, and Democracy*, 3d ed. (New York: Harper and Brothers Publishers, 1950), 132.

27. Schumpeter provides the following apt description of the entrepreneur: "To act with confidence beyond the range of familiar beacons and to overcome ... resistance requires aptitudes that are present in only a small fraction of the population and that define the entrepreneurial type as well as the entrepreneurial function." Ibid.

28. G. J. Wenham, J. A. Motyer, D. A. Carson, and R. T. France, eds., *New Bible Commentary, Twenty-First Century Edition* (Downers Grove, Ill.: InterVarsity Press, 1997), 938.

29. Leopold Fonck, *The Parables of the Gospel: An Exegetical and Practical Explanation*, 3d ed., ed. George O'Neill, trans. E. Leahy (New York: F. Pustet, 1914 [1902]), 542.

30. According to the teaching of Rabbi Gemara, "Samuel said: Money can only be guarded [by placing it] in the earth. Said Raba: Yet Samuel admits that on Sabbath eve at twilight the Rabbis did not put one to that trouble. Yet if he tarried after the conclusion of the

Sabbath long enough to bury it [the money] but omitted to do so, he is responsible [if it is stolen]." *The Babylonian Talmud* (Seder Nezikin), *Baba Metzia*, vol. 1, trans. H. Freedman (New York: Rebecca Bennet Publications Inc., 1959), 250–51. Also see the very next section (254–59) for a detailed discussion of liability surrounding the deposit of money with a bailiff, private individual, or third party.

31. Israel M. Kirzner, *Competition and Entrepreneurship* (Chicago: University of Chicago Press, 1973), 33.

32. Kirzner points out that entrepreneurial responses to changes in information should not be understood as a process of calculation. Rather, the entrepreneurial dimension concerns that element of a decision involving "a shrewd and wise assessment of the realities (both present and future) within the context of which the decision must be made." *Discovery and the Capitalist Process* (Chicago: University of Chicago Press, 1985), 17. Samuel Gregg comments incisively on Kirzner's statement: "'Assessment' is the key word here. It highlights the reality that each person's knowledge is limited and that each individual's acts consequently take place in, and contribute to, a context of uncertainty. For if there were no uncertainty, decision making would merely call for the precise calculation of facts and options, in which case, humans would be nothing more than robots. The reality is, however, that no matter how accurate one's calculations, a decision will be poor if its entrepreneurial-speculative component involves poor judgment." "The Rediscovery of Entrepreneurship: Developments in the Catholic Tradition," in *Christianity and Entrepreneurship: Protestant and Catholic Thoughts* (Australia: Center for Independent Studies, 1999), 65.

33. Monasteries were originally conceived to be a refuge from worldly concerns and a place where spiritual matters dominated daily life. Medieval monasteries were regulated by a constitution or set of internal rules, which, among other things, required that vows of chastity, poverty, and obedience be taken by the monks. One of the most widespread constitutions was the Rule of Saint Benedict, which applied to both the Benedictine and Cistercian Orders. This rule set forth specific guidelines that controlled the organization

and operation of monasteries and regulated the daily activities of the monks. For a recent translation with an excellent introduction and explanatory notes, see *The Rule of Saint Benedict*, trans. Anthony C. Meisel and M. L. del Mastro (Garden City, N.Y.: Image Books, 1975).

34. Robert B. Ekelund, Jr., Robert F. Hébert, Robert D. Tollison, Gary M. Anderson, and Audrey B. Davidson, *Sacred Trust: The Medieval Church As an Economic Firm* (New York: Oxford University Press, 1996), 53–54.

35. The Second Vatican Council's Decree on the Apostolate of Lay People (November 18, 1965) expands this argument in the following lengthy quotation:

> That men, working in harmony, should renew the temporal order and make it increasingly more perfect: Such is God's design for the world.
>
> All that goes to make up the temporal order: personal and family values, culture, economic interests, the trades and professions, institutions of the political community, international relations, and so on, as well as their gradual development—all these are not merely helps to man's last end; they possess a value of their own, placed in them by God, whether considered individually or as parts of the integral temporal structure: "And God saw all that he had made and found in very good" (Gen. 1:31). This natural goodness of theirs receives an added dignity from their relation with the human person, for whose use they have been created. And then, too, God has willed to gather together all that was natural, all that was supernatural, into a single whole in Christ, "so that in everything he would have the primacy" (Col. 1:18). Far from depriving the temporal order of its autonomy, of its specific ends, of its own laws and resources, or its importance for human well-being, this design, on the contrary, increases its energy and excellence, raising it at the same time to the level of man's integral vocation here below (no. 7).

About the Authors

ROBERT A. SIRICO is a Roman Catholic priest and the co-founder and President of the Acton Institute for the Study of Religion and Liberty.

WILLIAM E. LAMOTHE is Chairman Emeritus of the Kellogg Corporation in Battle Creek, Michigan.